WHAT MAKES US

Sisters

WHAT MAKES US

Sisters

Bonnie L. Oscarson

DESERET
BOOK

SALT LAKE CITY, UTAH

Library of Congress Cataloging-in-Publication Data
(CIP data on file)
ISBN 978-1-62972-041-8

Printed in Canada
Friesens, Manitoba, Canada
10   9   8   7   6   5   4   3   2   1

To all of the women who have blessed my life—
beginning with my amazing mother,
Jean Stringham Green

WE REJOICE in our many different roles as women in the Church. Though in many ways we are different and unique, we also acknowledge that we are all daughters of the same Heavenly Father, which makes us *sisters*.

We are *unified* in building the kingdom of God and in the covenants we have made, no matter what our circumstances.

To be sisters implies that there is an UNBREAKABLE BOND between us. Sisters *take care* of each other, *watch out* for each other, *comfort* each other, and are there for each other through thick and thin. The Lord has said,

"I say unto you, be one; and if ye are not one ye are not mine."

D&C 38:27

THE ADVERSARY

would have us
be *critical* or
judgmental
of one another.

He wants us to concentrate on our *differences* and *compare ourselves* to one another.

Some may love to exercise vigorously for an hour each day because it makes them feel so good, while others consider it to be a major athletic event if they walk up one flight of stairs instead of taking the elevator.

They can still be friends,
can't they?

Women can be *especially hard* on themselves. When we compare ourselves to one another, we will always feel inadequate or resentful of others.

SISTER PATRICIA T. HOLLAND once said, "The point is, we simply cannot call ourselves Christian and continue to *judge* one another—or ourselves—so harshly." She goes on to say that there is nothing that is worth losing our compassion and sisterhood over. We just need to relax and rejoice in our *divine differences*. We need to realize that we all desire to serve in the kingdom, using our unique talents and gifts in our own ways.

Then we can
enjoy our
sisterhood and
our associations
and begin to
serve.

The fact of the matter is that we really and truly *need* each other.

Women naturally seek FRIENDSHIP, SUPPORT, and COMPANIONSHIP.

We have SO MUCH TO LEARN from one another, and we often let self-imposed barriers keep us from enjoying associations that could be among the *greatest blessings* in our lives.

For example, women who are a little older need what Primary-age girls have to offer. *Those young girls have so much to teach about Christlike service and love.*

A little girl named *Sarah*, along with her mother, had the opportunity to help a woman in her ward named *Brenda*, who had multiple sclerosis.

SARAH LOVED TO GO with her mother to help Brenda. She would put lotion on Brenda's hands and massage her fingers and arms, which were often in pain. Sarah then learned to gently stretch Brenda's arms over her head to exercise her muscles. Sarah brushed Brenda's hair and visited with her while her mother took care of Brenda's other needs.

Sarah learned the *importance* and *joy* of serving another person and came to understand that

even a child can make a

big difference

in someone's life.

I love the example in the first chapter of Luke, which describes the sweet relationship between *Mary,* the mother of Jesus, and her cousin *Elisabeth.*

Mary was a young woman when she was informed of her remarkable mission to be the mother of the Son of God. Initially it must have seemed to be a heavy responsibility to bear alone.

It was the Lord Himself who provided Mary with someone to *share her load*. Through the message of the angel Gabriel, Mary was given the name of a trusted and sympathetic woman to whom she could turn for *support*—her cousin Elisabeth.

This young maiden, *Mary,* and her cousin, who was "well stricken in years" (Luke 1:7), shared a common bond in their miraculous pregnancies, and I can only imagine how very important the three months they spent together were to both of them as they were able to *talk* together, *empathize* with each other, and *support* one another in their unique callings.

What a wonderful model they are of feminine nurturing between generations.

I ONCE ASKED my mother why in the world she did that week after week when she had no support or encouragement at home.

Her answer was, *"I had Primary teachers who loved me."* These teachers cared about her and taught her the gospel. They taught her that she had a Father in Heaven, who loved her, and it was their concern for her that kept her coming week after week. My mother said to me, "That was one of the most *important influences* in my early life."

I hope I can thank *those wonderful sisters someday!*

There is no AGE BARRIER when it comes to *Christlike* service.

I met a stake Young Women president in California who told me that her 81-YEAR-OLD mother had recently been called to be a Mia Maid adviser. I was so intrigued that I gave that mother a call. Sister Val Baker said that when her bishop had asked to meet with her, she was looking forward to being called as a librarian or ward historian. When he then asked her to serve as a Mia Maid adviser to the Young Women, her reaction was, *"Are you sure?"*

Her bishop solemnly replied, "Sister Baker, make no mistake; this call is from the Lord." She said she had no other answer to that except, "Of course."

I love the inspiration this bishop felt that the four Mia Maids in his ward would have *much to learn* from the wisdom, experience, and lifelong example of this mature sister. And guess whom Sister Baker will go to when she needs help setting up her Facebook page!

I think of the great help that the sisters in Relief Society can be in WELCOMING YOUNG SISTERS who have recently been in Young Women. Our young sisters frequently feel as if they don't have a place or anything in common with those in Relief Society. Before they turn eighteen, they need Young Women leaders and mothers who will joyfully testify of the great blessings of Relief Society. They need to feel enthusiastic about becoming part of such a *glorious organization.*

When young women begin attending Relief Society, what they need most is a *friend* to sit next to, an *arm* around their shoulders, and an *opportunity* to teach and serve.

Let us all reach out to help one
another through the transitions and
milestones of our lives.

Countless women of the Church are ***reaching out*** *across age and cultural lines to bless and serve others, and they deserve thanks.*

Young women are *serving* Primary children and the elderly. Single sisters of all ages spend countless hours watching out for the *needs* of those around them. Thousands of young women are giving up eighteen months of their lives to *share the gospel* with the world.

All of these things are evidence that,
as our beloved hymn states,

"The errand of *angels*
is given to women."

"As Sisters in Zion," *Hymns,* no. 309

If there are barriers, it is because
we have created them. We must STOP
concentrating on our *differences* and
look for what we have in *common*;

then we can begin to realize our

greatest potential

and achieve the greatest
good in this world.

SISTER MARJORIE P. HINCKLEY once said, "Oh, how we need each other. Those of us who are *old* need you who are young. And, hopefully, you who are *young* need some of us who are old. It is a sociological fact that women need women. We need deep and satisfying and loyal friendships with each other."

Sister Hinckley was right; oh, how we need each other!

There is no other group of women in the world who have access to GREATER BLESSINGS than Latter-day Saint women.

We are members of the Lord's Church, and regardless of our individual circumstances, we can all enjoy the full blessings of *priesthood power* through keeping the covenants we have made at baptism and in the temple.

We have *living prophets* to lead and teach us, and we enjoy the great gift of the *Holy Ghost,* which serves as a comfort and guide in our lives. We are blessed to work hand in hand with righteous brothers as we strengthen homes and families.

We have access to the
strength and power of
temple ordinances
and so much more.

IN ADDITION to enjoying all of these magnificent blessings, we have *each other*—sisters in the gospel of Jesus Christ. We have been blessed with tender and charitable natures, which enable us to render *Christlike love* and service to those around us.

As we look beyond our differences in age, culture, and circumstance to nurture and serve one another,

we will be filled with the

pure love of Christ

and the inspiration that leads us to know when and whom to serve.

I extend to each sister in the gospel an invitation that was issued once before by a Relief Society general president.

SISTER BONNIE D. PARKIN said, "I invite you to not only love each other more but love each other *better*."

May we realize just how much we need each other, and may we all love *one another better, is my prayer.*

This book is based on Sister Oscarson's April 2014 general women's session address, "Sisterhood: Oh, How We Need Each Other." At the request of Deseret Book, the talk has been adapted for general publication.

NOTES

Patricia T. Holland, "'One Thing Needful': Becoming Women of Greater Faith in Christ," *Ensign,* Oct. 1987, 29.

Glimpses into the Life and Heart of Marjorie Pay Hinckley, ed. Virginia H. Pearce (1999), 254–55.

Bonnie D. Parkin, "Choosing Charity: That Good Part," *Ensign* or *Liahona,* Nov. 2003, 106.

PHOTO CREDITS